SECRETS of the DEEP
REVEALED

Written by
DR. FRANCES DIPPER

DK Publishing

LONDON, NEW YORK, MUNICH,
MELBOURNE, and DELHI

SENIOR EDITOR CAREY SCOTT
SENIOR ART EDITOR JOANNE CONNOR
EDITORS CLAIRE WATTS, SARAH GOULDING
DESIGNER JOANNE LITTLE
PHOTOSHOP ILLUSTRATOR LEE GIBBONS
MANAGING EDITOR CAMILLA HALLINAN
MANAGING ART EDITOR SOPHIA MTT
CATEGORY PUBLISHER SUE GRABHAM
ART DIRECTOR MARK RICHARDS
PICTURE RESEARCHER JO DE GRAY
JACKET DESIGNER CHRIS DREW
JACKET EDITOR BETH APPLE
DTP DESIGNER JILL BUNYAN
PRODUCTION CONTROLLER DULCIE ROWE

First American Edition, 2003

Published in the United States by
DK Publishing, Inc.
375 Hudson Street
New York, New York 10014

04 05 06 07 08 10 9 8 7 6 5 4 3 2

A Cataloging-in-Publication record for this book
is available from the Library of Congress.

ISBN 0-7894-9272-5

Color reproduction by Colourscan, Singapore
Printed in China by Leo Paper Products

See our complete product line at
www.dk.com

CONTENTS

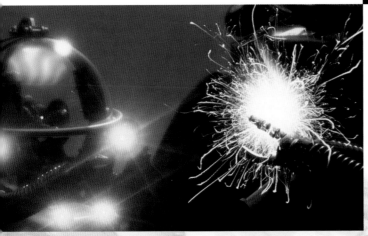

DIVING DOWN
When the first diving suits appeared in the 17th century, they were supplied with air from the surface using a bellows and a flexible pipe. The invention of the aqualung in the 1940s changed everything—now divers could swim freely with their own supply of compressed air in tanks on their backs.

WHAT LIES BENEATH

BENEATH THE SEA lies a fascinating and mysterious hidden world. In the past, sailors thought that the ocean might be bottomless. Deep-sea creatures dredged up in fishermen's nets were so different from land species that they seemed like hideous monsters. Today, advances in technology have begun to unravel the ocean's mysteries. Sonar enables us to measure the ocean's depths, create maps of the ocean floor, and even find ancient wrecks lying on the seabed. Modern diving equipment and submersibles allow people to enter the deep-sea world to watch underwater animals and plants in their natural environment. However, the oceans cover such a vast area of the Earth's surface that even with this modern equipment, the underwater world still holds many secrets that scientists have not yet uncovered.

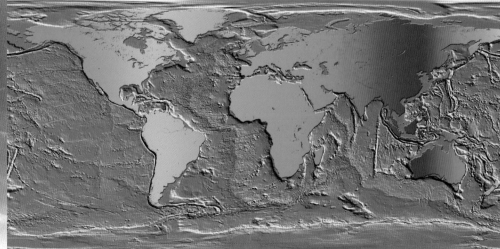

SWIMMING FREE
Today's modern diving equipment is so reliable and easy to use that it takes very little training to master. It is safe to dive with an aqualung to depths of about 130 ft (40 m).

OCEAN FLOOR TOPOGRAPHY
The oceans cover more than two-thirds of the surface of the Earth. Modern sonar technology has produced maps of the hidden landscape of mountain ranges, plains, deep ocean trenches, and volcanoes beneath the ever-moving waters.

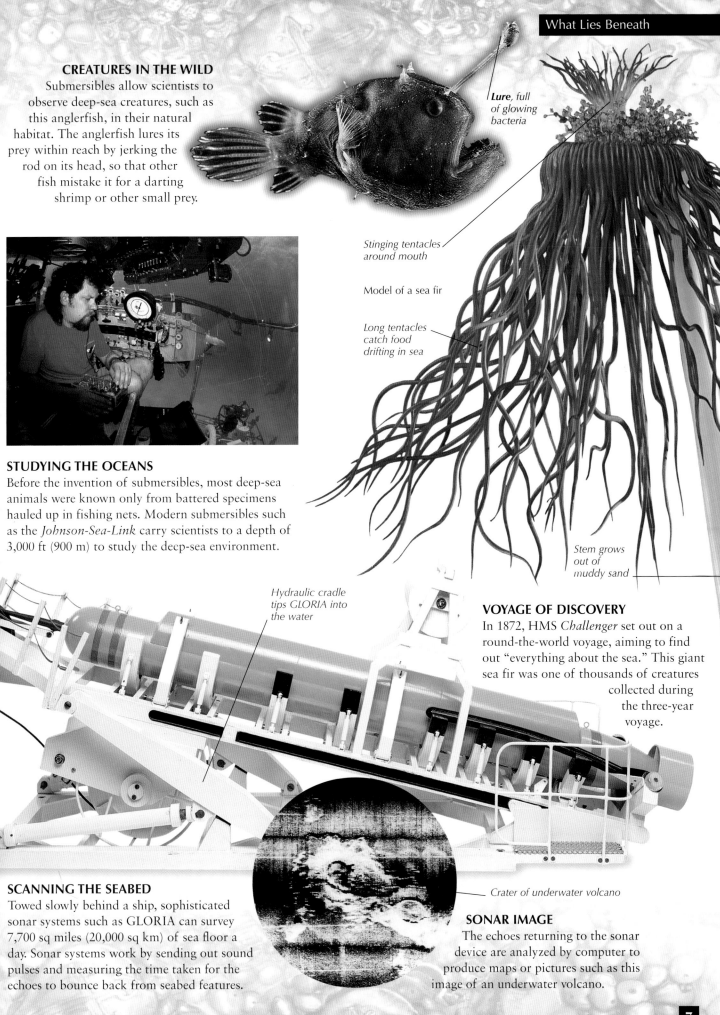

CREATURES IN THE WILD

Submersibles allow scientists to observe deep-sea creatures, such as this anglerfish, in their natural habitat. The anglerfish lures its prey within reach by jerking the rod on its head, so that other fish mistake it for a darting shrimp or other small prey.

Lure, full of glowing bacteria

Stinging tentacles around mouth

Model of a sea fir

Long tentacles catch food drifting in sea

STUDYING THE OCEANS

Before the invention of submersibles, most deep-sea animals were known only from battered specimens hauled up in fishing nets. Modern submersibles such as the *Johnson-Sea-Link* carry scientists to a depth of 3,000 ft (900 m) to study the deep-sea environment.

Stem grows out of muddy sand

Hydraulic cradle tips GLORIA into the water

VOYAGE OF DISCOVERY

In 1872, HMS *Challenger* set out on a round-the-world voyage, aiming to find out "everything about the sea." This giant sea fir was one of thousands of creatures collected during the three-year voyage.

SCANNING THE SEABED

Towed slowly behind a ship, sophisticated sonar systems such as GLORIA can survey 7,700 sq miles (20,000 sq km) of sea floor a day. Sonar systems work by sending out sound pulses and measuring the time taken for the echoes to bounce back from seabed features.

Crater of underwater volcano

SONAR IMAGE

The echoes returning to the sonar device are analyzed by computer to produce maps or pictures such as this image of an underwater volcano.

THE TITANIC

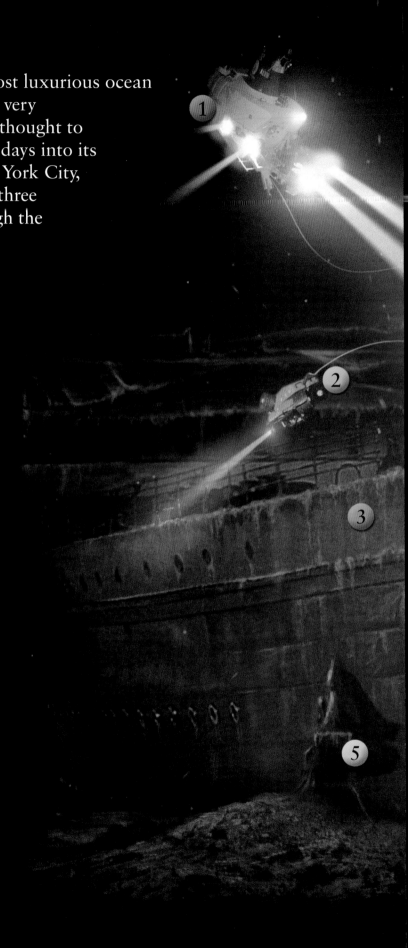

THE *TITANIC* WAS the biggest, most luxurious ocean liner ever built. Fitted with the very latest in safety features, it was thought to be virtually unsinkable. Yet only four days into its maiden voyage from England to New York City, the *Titanic* struck an iceberg. Within three short hours it was plummeting through the icy ocean, taking 1,490 lives with it. Here on the ocean floor it lay undetected for 73 years. The *Titanic*'s position was discovered in 1985 by an expedition led by Robert Ballard. A year later, Ballard dived down to the site in the submersible *Alvin* and, with a remote-controlled underwater camera, *Jason Junior*, was able to film inside the wreck.

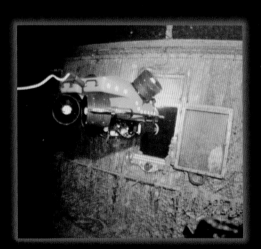

FADED SPLENDOR
The lights of *Jason Junior* show only a thick covering of silt and rust as it peers through a broken window. The "swimming eyeball" is looking into the remains of a first-class stateroom, once the height of opulence.

THE TITANIC

THE *TITANIC* WAS the biggest, most luxurious ocean liner ever built. Fitted with the very latest in safety features, it was thought to be virtually unsinkable. Yet only four days into its maiden voyage from England to New York City, the *Titanic* struck an iceberg. Within three short hours it was plummeting through the icy ocean, taking 1,490 lives with it. Here on the ocean floor it lay undetected for 73 years. The *Titanic*'s position was discovered in 1985 by an expedition led by Robert Ballard. A year later, Ballard dived down to the site in the submersible *Alvin* and, with a remote-controlled underwater camera, *Jason Junior*, was able to film inside the wreck.

FADED SPLENDOR
The lights of *Jason Junior* show only a thick covering of silt and rust as it peers through a broken window. The "swimming eyeball" is looking into the remains of a first-class stateroom, once the height of opulence.

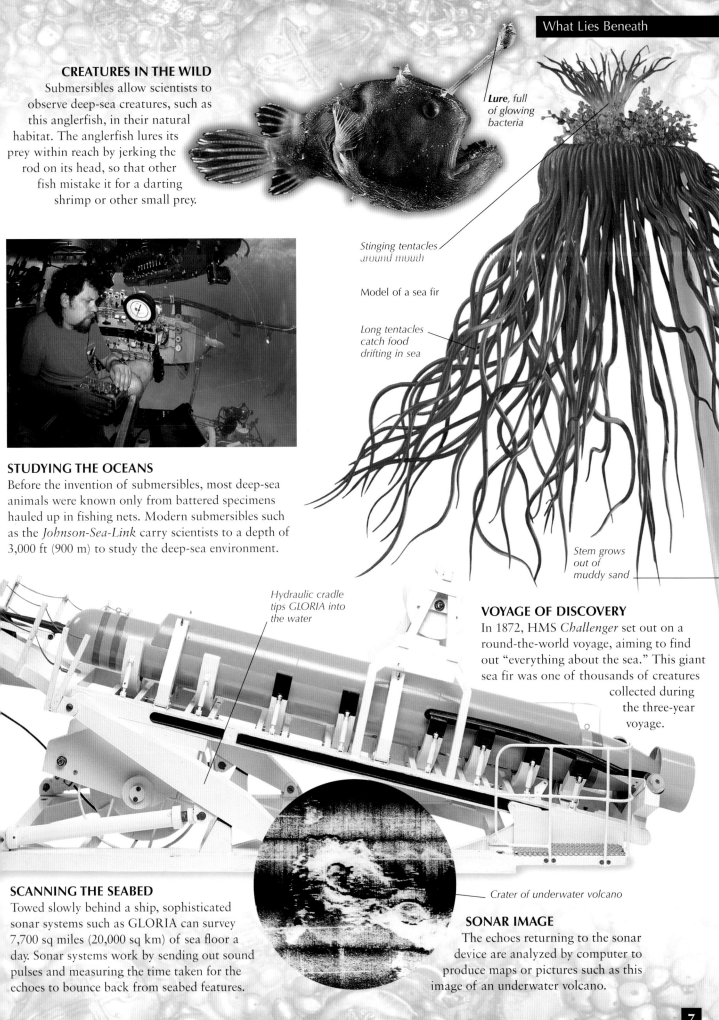

CREATURES IN THE WILD

Submersibles allow scientists to observe deep-sea creatures, such as this anglerfish, in their natural habitat. The anglerfish lures its prey within reach by jerking the rod on its head, so that other fish mistake it for a darting shrimp or other small prey.

Lure, full of glowing bacteria

Stinging tentacles around mouth

Model of a sea fir

Long tentacles catch food drifting in sea

STUDYING THE OCEANS

Before the invention of submersibles, most deep-sea animals were known only from battered specimens hauled up in fishing nets. Modern submersibles such as the *Johnson-Sea-Link* carry scientists to a depth of 3,000 ft (900 m) to study the deep-sea environment.

Stem grows out of muddy sand

Hydraulic cradle tips GLORIA into the water

VOYAGE OF DISCOVERY

In 1872, HMS *Challenger* set out on a round-the-world voyage, aiming to find out "everything about the sea." This giant sea fir was one of thousands of creatures collected during the three-year voyage.

SCANNING THE SEABED

Towed slowly behind a ship, sophisticated sonar systems such as GLORIA can survey 7,700 sq miles (20,000 sq km) of sea floor a day. Sonar systems work by sending out sound pulses and measuring the time taken for the echoes to bounce back from seabed features.

Crater of underwater volcano

SONAR IMAGE

The echoes returning to the sonar device are analyzed by computer to produce maps or pictures such as this image of an underwater volcano.

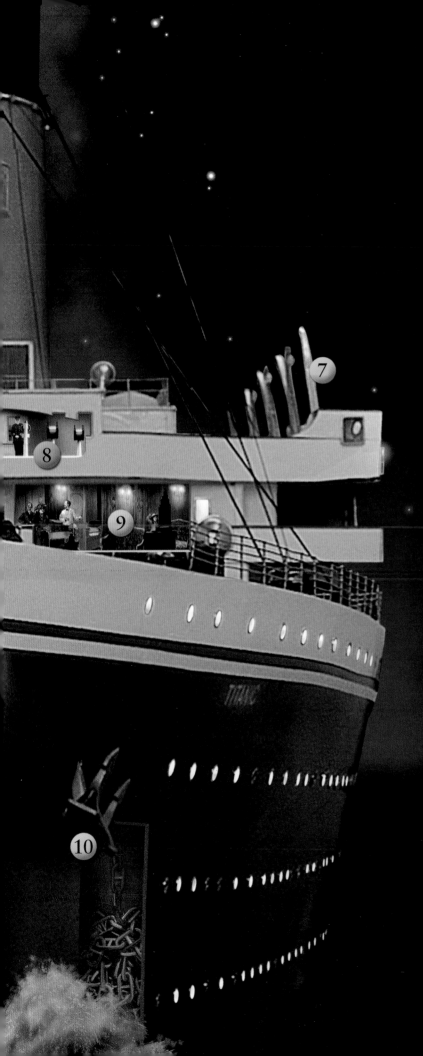

EXPLORING THE TITANIC

1. **Alvin:** *the first submersible to explore the wreck*

2. **Jason Junior:** *operated via a fiber-optic control cable, 250 ft (77.5 m) long*

3. **Bow:** *the bow section remains upright and relatively intact*

4. **Rusticles:** *rust hangs off the bow in long ribbons created by iron-eating bacteria*

5. **Starboard anchor:** *one of two main anchors, each weighing 16 tons*

6. **Lookout:** *Frederick Fleet, the lookout, spotted the iceberg, but it was too late*

7. **Davits:** *for lowering the lifeboats. Only one in three passengers were saved*

8. **The bridge:** *Captain J. Smith commanded the ship from here*

9. **Stateroom:** *first-class staterooms were below the bridge*

10. **Port anchor:** *the chain was 330 fathoms (2,000 ft/615 m) long*

GRAND STAIRCASE

The remains of a crystal chandelier lie on the decayed floor of the ship. Some first-class areas, including the splendid Grand Staircase, were lit by several such chandeliers. The lights, elegant glass dome, oak-paneled walls, and heavily carved balustrade made the staircase one of the *Titanic*'s most lavish features.

LOW-TECH SEARCH

To narrow down the search area, Robert Ballard and his team carefully studied maps and charts detailing the *Titanic*'s position before sinking and the position where the lifeboats were found. The *Titanic* was eventually found 13 miles (21 km) from the position where it was thought to have sunk.

Robert Ballard

SCANNING THE SEABED

Ballard and his French partner Jean-Louis Michel started the search with a French ship, *Le Suroit*, towing this sonar instrument back and forth over the seabed. The sonar device scanned three-quarters of the search area before the US ship *Knorr* took over.

MISSION TITANIC

WHEN THE *TITANIC* sank in 1912, ships did not have very accurate position-fixing equipment, so the exact spot where it went down was not known. Robert Ballard was convinced that previous missions to find the ship had failed because they had not covered a wide enough area. For his expedition, two ships examined a 100-square-mile (260-sq-km) area of the Atlantic. Time was running out and bad weather was closing in, when at last the *Titanic* was spotted. When Ballard finished surveying the ship in 1986, he left a plaque aboard the *Titanic* in memory of those who had died, hoping the wreck would be left in peace. But the *Titanic* did not lie undisturbed for long—later expeditions have recovered many fascinating objects from this extraordinarily well-preserved wreck.

ARGO

The *Titanic* was finally located using this steel sled, called *Argo*, which was towed along behind the surface ship *Knorr*. *Argo* was fitted with video cameras that filmed the sea floor and sent the moving pictures up the tow cable to video screens on the ship. On the return trip in 1986, *Argo* also took 57,000 still photographs of the wreckage.

Video cameras
to relay pictures to the surface ship

THE BOILER

At about one o'clock in the morning on September 1, 1985, *Argo* began to send back images of a trail of manufactured objects. Then something large and perfectly round appeared—it was one of the ship's 29 massive boilers. *Titanic* had been found at last!

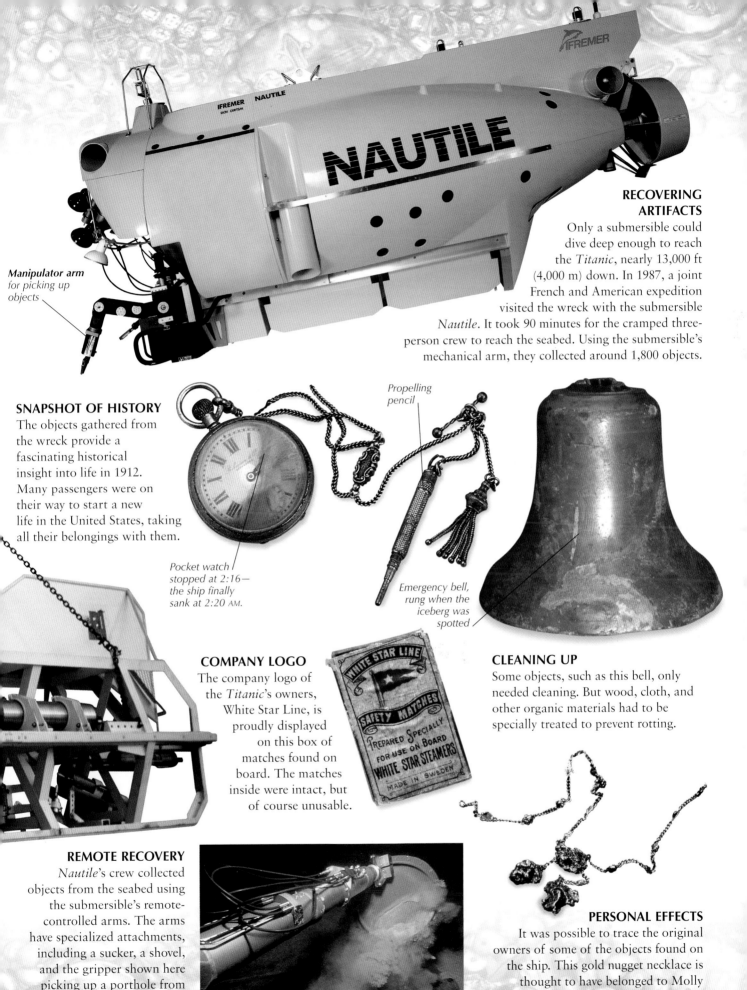

Manipulator arm
for picking up objects

RECOVERING ARTIFACTS

Only a submersible could dive deep enough to reach the *Titanic*, nearly 13,000 ft (4,000 m) down. In 1987, a joint French and American expedition visited the wreck with the submersible *Nautile*. It took 90 minutes for the cramped three-person crew to reach the seabed. Using the submersible's mechanical arm, they collected around 1,800 objects.

SNAPSHOT OF HISTORY

The objects gathered from the wreck provide a fascinating historical insight into life in 1912. Many passengers were on their way to start a new life in the United States, taking all their belongings with them.

Propelling pencil

Pocket watch stopped at 2:16— the ship finally sank at 2:20 AM.

Emergency bell, rung when the iceberg was spotted

COMPANY LOGO

The company logo of the *Titanic*'s owners, White Star Line, is proudly displayed on this box of matches found on board. The matches inside were intact, but of course unusable.

WHITE STAR LINE

SAFETY MATCHES

PREPARED SPECIALLY FOR USE ON BOARD WHITE STAR STEAMERS

MADE IN SWEDEN

CLEANING UP

Some objects, such as this bell, only needed cleaning. But wood, cloth, and other organic materials had to be specially treated to prevent rotting.

REMOTE RECOVERY

Nautile's crew collected objects from the seabed using the submersible's remote-controlled arms. The arms have specialized attachments, including a sucker, a shovel, and the gripper shown here picking up a porthole from the seabed.

PERSONAL EFFECTS

It was possible to trace the original owners of some of the objects found on the ship. This gold nugget necklace is thought to have belonged to Molly Brown, a survivor of the wreck.

TREASURE TROVE

During a hurricane in 1724, a beautiful Spanish galleon called the *Conde de Tolosa* sank on a coral reef off the coast of the Dominican Republic in the Caribbean. When salvage divers located the ship in 1977, they found real treasure—pearls, silver, and rare pieces of diamond-studded gold jewelry.

These pearls were surprisingly uncorroded after their long immersion in sea water

OCEAN TREASURES

IN THE MID-1930S, a fisherman off the port of Vung Tau in Vietnam pulled in his nets and found not the red snapper he was hoping for, but a lump of ancient iron and porcelain. He had discovered the wreck of a 17th-century Chinese junk, full of valuable china and other trade goods. Divers and fishermen often dream of finding a shipwreck packed with treasure like this, but most are found by professional salvage companies. Even if the wreck has rotted on the seabed for centuries, its cargo still belongs to someone. Salvage divers must pay the rightful owners a proportion of the value of everything recovered.

Stacks of coins fused together

CLEANING UP COINS

Seawater is very corrosive, so when coins and other treasures are brought up from a wreck, they are often stuck together with rust and other deposits, in a lump called a concretion. It takes hours to separate and clean the individual coins, first using a chisel to chip away at the concretion, then soaking them in chemicals.

Coins after cleaning process

Vung Tau china, among the first made for export to Europe

PRECIOUS PORCELAIN

Chinese junks like the one found off Vung Tau were big ocean-going ships used to carry cargoes of porcelain chinaware, often destined for Europe. The Vung Tau salvage team recovered over 48,000 pieces of crockery and other objects. 28,000 pieces of the china were sold for a staggering $7 million.

FIRE!

For hundreds of years, junks were the largest, safest ships on the seas. But no ship is unsinkable. When the Vung Tau wreck was excavated, archaeologists could see why it had sunk—charred beams down to its waterline showed that there had been a fire on board.

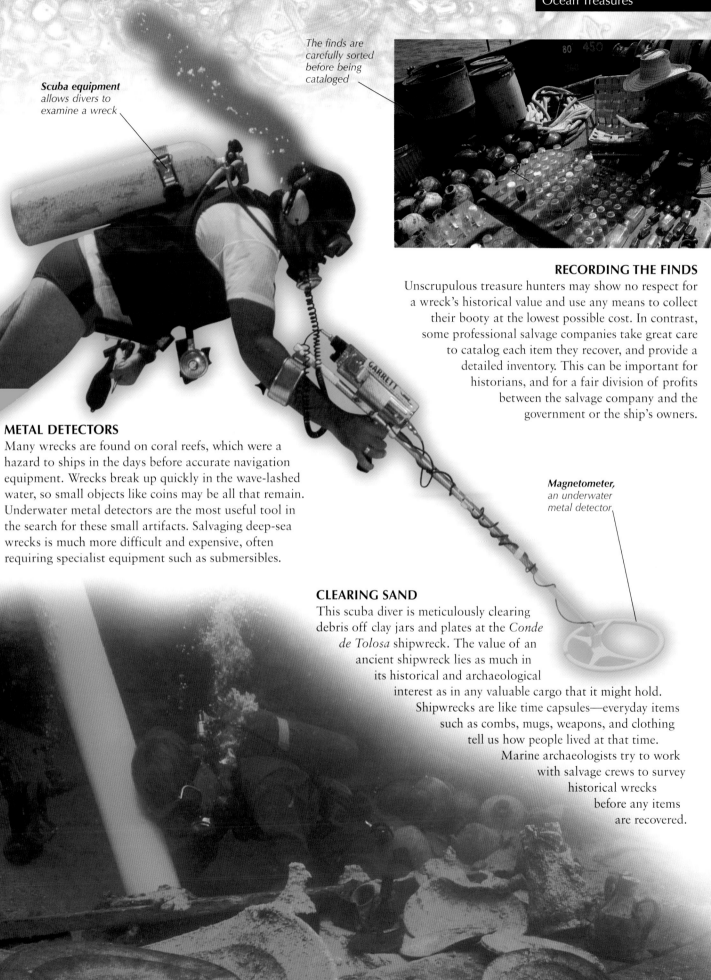

Scuba equipment allows divers to examine a wreck

The finds are carefully sorted before being cataloged

RECORDING THE FINDS

Unscrupulous treasure hunters may show no respect for a wreck's historical value and use any means to collect their booty at the lowest possible cost. In contrast, some professional salvage companies take great care to catalog each item they recover, and provide a detailed inventory. This can be important for historians, and for a fair division of profits between the salvage company and the government or the ship's owners.

METAL DETECTORS

Many wrecks are found on coral reefs, which were a hazard to ships in the days before accurate navigation equipment. Wrecks break up quickly in the wave-lashed water, so small objects like coins may be all that remain. Underwater metal detectors are the most useful tool in the search for these small artifacts. Salvaging deep-sea wrecks is much more difficult and expensive, often requiring specialist equipment such as submersibles.

Magnetometer, an underwater metal detector

CLEARING SAND

This scuba diver is meticulously clearing debris off clay jars and plates at the *Conde de Tolosa* shipwreck. The value of an ancient shipwreck lies as much in its historical and archaeological interest as in any valuable cargo that it might hold. Shipwrecks are like time capsules—everyday items such as combs, mugs, weapons, and clothing tell us how people lived at that time. Marine archaeologists try to work with salvage crews to survey historical wrecks before any items are recovered.

MAPPING A WRECK SITE
Marine archaeologists make detailed maps of the site of an important historical wreck, such as this ship, popularly known as the *Glass Wreck*, which sank off Turkey in the 11th century. By labeling the artifacts and mapping their positions, the archaeologists can figure out what the ship looked like.

MAPPING THE OCEAN

MOST OF THE EARTH'S land masses have been mapped using photographs from airplanes and satellites. We even have maps of the Moon. But only around a tenth of the ocean floor has been mapped in detail because, even in the clearest seas, it is impossible to see much of the seabed from the surface. So scientists have developed a system called sonar, which uses sound signals to build up a picture of the ocean floor. Sonar can also be used to search for wrecks. Once found, the exact position of a seabed feature or wreck can be recorded using a Global Positioning System (GPS) unit. Then divers can relocate the site to investigate the find and make detailed maps.

FINDING *MARY ROSE*
The *Mary Rose* was King Henry VIII of England's flagship. In 1967, 437 years after it sank, the ship was relocated by sonar equipment. The wreck was gradually excavated by archaeologists and volunteer divers.

Jets constantly spray the wreck with a water-based wax solution to preserve the timbers

MAPPING *MARY ROSE*
The *Mary Rose* sank in 1545 during a fierce fight with the French near Portsmouth, off the south coast of England. When the ship was discovered, the remains of its hull were buried in the muddy seabed. The excavation uncovered more than 16,000 objects, including tools, navigational equipment, clothing, food, and guns. By mapping the exact positions of the guns on the ship, archaeologists uncovered new information about how such ships fought. Every timber was carefully measured before the hull was finally raised to the surface in 1982.

SATELLITE SIGNALS

Satellites in space can measure the color, temperature, and slope (height) of the sea surface. From these measurements, computers can calculate and map the ocean currents, shallow and deep areas, and wind speed, and transmit this information to oceanographers.

GPS units enable ships to pinpoint their position at sea to within a few yards, allowing modern sailors to navigate much more accurately than in the past.

POSITION SECURE

A GPS satellite orbits the Earth at the same speed as the Earth rotates, so the satellite always stays in the same position above the Earth's surface. GPS units on board ships pick up signals from several GPS satellites. The GPS unit works out how far the ship is from the fixed position of each satellite, and uses these measurements to calculate the ship's exact position at sea.

Blue areas are 10,000 ft (3,000 m) below sea level

Orange plateaus are 3,300 ft (1,000 m) below sea level

MAPPING THE SEABED

Sonar has been used to create this map of the continental shelf off California. Sonar works by sending out pulses of sound and measuring the time taken for the echoes to bounce back. A computer converts the data into a map, using colors to represent different depths.

White areas are at sea level

DEEPSEA VIEW

DEEP SUBMERGENCE VEHICLES (DSVs), such as the US Navy's *Alvin*, carry scientists to the darkest depths of the world's oceans. Some can dive as far down as 4 miles (6.5 km) to a world never seen before. Scientists knew that there were strange fish and other creatures living at these depths—but until *Alvin* and other submersibles were developed, no one had seen them alive in their natural habitat. Today, amazing deep-sea life—such as glowing jellyfish and fish with monstrous jaws and bizarre, light-emitting organs—can be seen and filmed by the brave explorers inside these cramped capsules.

DSV *ALVIN*
Just 23 ft (7 m) long, *Alvin* carries one pilot and two observers. They operate the external cameras, two manipulators (robotic "arms"), and a sled equipped with instruments such as water samplers and probes.

EXPLORING THE DEPTHS

1. **Data-logging computer:** *logs all scientific, tracking, and navigation data*

2. **Underwater telephone:** *keeps the crew in constant contact with the surface ship*

3. **Oxygen monitors:** *alarms flash to indicate high or low concentrations of oxygen*

4. **Starboard manipulator control:** *operates a hydraulic arm at the front of the vessel*

5. **Viperfish:** *up to 12 in (30 cm) long, it is invisible until it opens its jaws—then 350 tiny light organs lure its prey inside*

6. **Fangtooth:** *up to 6 in (15 cm) long, it eats anything, and is also known as the ogrefish*

7. **Black sea dragon:** *up to 16 in (40 cm) long, only the female has teeth and a luminous barbel (lure) on her chin to attract prey*

8. **Umbrella gulper eel:** *up to 30 in (75 cm) long, it opens its mouth wide to scoop up its prey*

9. **Port manipulator:** *attachment slurps up a deep-sea jellyfish for study at the surface*

10. **Starboard manipulator:** *extends up to 75 in (2 m) and lifts up to 250 lb (113 kg)*

ALLURING ANGLER
An anglerfish extends its lure (a "fishing line" with a luminous tip) to capture passing prey. With its cavernous mouth and expandable stomach, the anglerfish can swallow prey as big as itself.

CRITTERCAM

In 1986, scientists came up with an extraordinary way to explore the Antarctic Ocean, deep beneath the ice where no submersible or diver can safely go. They attached a tiny camera, called a Crittercam, to a Weddell seal, then released the seal through a specially cut ice-hole. When the seal returned to the hole to breathe, the scientists retrieved the camera and its unique images of Antarctic ocean life.

Fluid-filled joints allow three-fourths of normal mobility

UNDER PRESSURE

DEEP IN THE OCEAN, the weight of the water above creates huge pressure—at the lowest depths, building up to more than 1,000 times the surface pressure. The human body cannot withstand such pressure, and unprotected divers can only reach depths of about 1,800 ft (550 m). To reach even these depths, must use special breathing equipment and undergo lengthy decompression afterward. To avoid such problems, divers have to wear pressure-resistant suits to protect their bodies. A submersible can carry people to greater depths, but the safest way to explore and work in the ocean's depths is by using an unmanned submersible called an ROV (Remotely Operated Vehicle).

Wetsuit, for warmth at great depths

Hydraulic pincers act as hands

FREE DIVING

This diver is taking part in a competition to see how deep he can dive with just a lungful of air. The current record, set in August 2002, is 525 ft (160 m). It is doubtful whether this record can be extended much further. At this depth the diver's lungs are squashed to less than one-sixteenth of their normal size by the water pressure, and the chest is in danger of caving in.

PRESSURE SUITS

One way for divers to avoid the effects of pressure is to wear suits that keep them at surface pressure. However, these "personal submarines" have to be made from strong, rigid materials to prevent the suit (and the diver inside) from being crushed by the increasing pressure as they go down. This means that the suits are heavy and ungainly, and only used for specialized survey work.

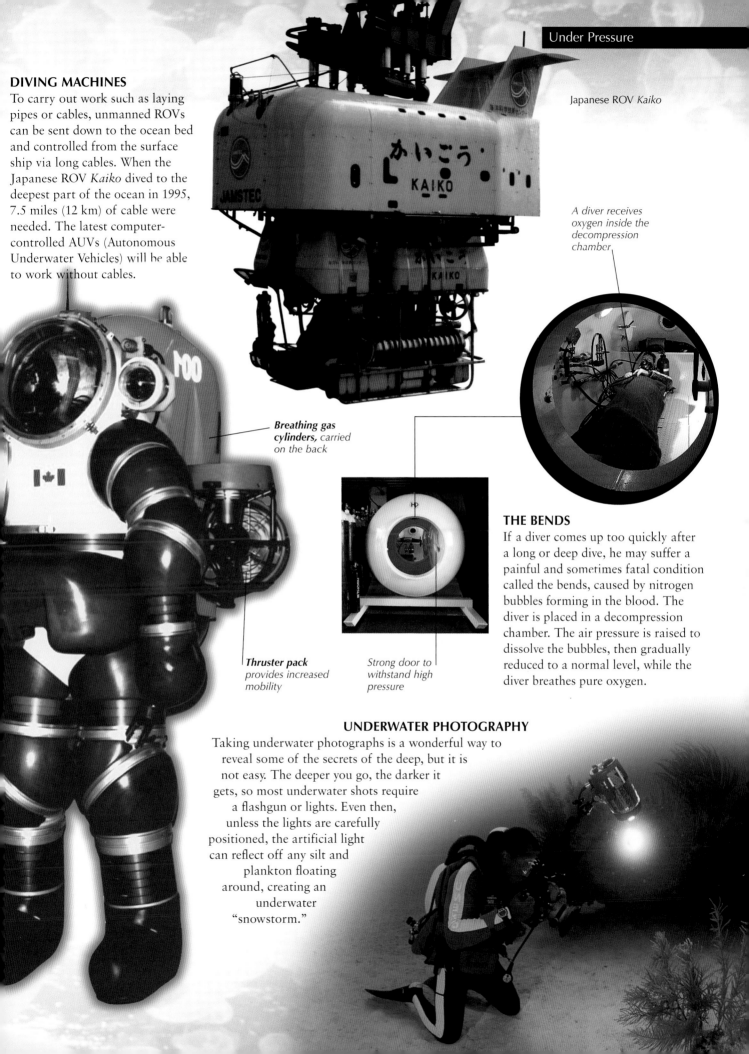

DIVING MACHINES

To carry out work such as laying pipes or cables, unmanned ROVs can be sent down to the ocean bed and controlled from the surface ship via long cables. When the Japanese ROV *Kaiko* dived to the deepest part of the ocean in 1995, 7.5 miles (12 km) of cable were needed. The latest computer-controlled AUVs (Autonomous Underwater Vehicles) will be able to work without cables.

Japanese ROV *Kaiko*

A diver receives oxygen inside the decompression chamber

Breathing gas cylinders, *carried on the back*

Thruster pack *provides increased mobility*

Strong door to withstand high pressure

THE BENDS

If a diver comes up too quickly after a long or deep dive, he may suffer a painful and sometimes fatal condition called the bends, caused by nitrogen bubbles forming in the blood. The diver is placed in a decompression chamber. The air pressure is raised to dissolve the bubbles, then gradually reduced to a normal level, while the diver breathes pure oxygen.

UNDERWATER PHOTOGRAPHY

Taking underwater photographs is a wonderful way to reveal some of the secrets of the deep, but it is not easy. The deeper you go, the darker it gets, so most underwater shots require a flashgun or lights. Even then, unless the lights are carefully positioned, the artificial light can reflect off any silt and plankton floating around, creating an underwater "snowstorm."

JELLY FISHING

Jellyfish are very common in the mid-water world, where there is no surface and no bottom. The shape of this bell jelly helps it to float effortlessly while fishing for prey with its long tentacles. The tentacles are packed with stinging cells which shoot out barbed threads, like minute harpoons, into their prey. Baby fish, small shrimp, and other floating animals are caught and paralyzed in this way.

Tentacles are several times the length of the body

SEEING IS BELIEVING

IN THE DEEP SEA, the water is barely above freezing point, there is total darkness, and the water pressure would crush a human in an instant. But deep-sea fish have adapted to survive in this hostile environment. They do not feel the extreme pressure because they have no air spaces in their compact bodies. Many contain a chemical called trimethylamine oxide, which helps their bodies work under high pressure. Deep-sea fish do not feel the cold, either, because their body temperature matches that of the water. Many have also developed strange body features to help them find food and stay afloat at great depths.

FROZEN FISH

In the coldest parts of the ocean, the water temperature can fall to 30°F (–1.9°C) before it freezes. Most fish would die at these temperatures. But icefish blood has no red blood cells, which means it flows freely even in very cold conditions. A natural antifreeze in the icefish's blood means it can even survive being frozen in ice.

Glowing light organ beneath each eye can be turned on and off by covering with a flap of skin

Large, winglike pectoral fins for propulsion through the water

FLASHING LIGHTS

Sunlight only reaches down into the ocean to about 3,280 ft (1,000 m)—below this, it is inky black. Most of the animals living in this dark zone have overcome this problem by producing their own light, called bioluminescence. This flashlight fish goes one step further—it has a light organ that it can flash in order to confuse hungry predators.

BIG BELLY

Food is in short supply in the cold, dark depths of the ocean, so fish must be able to eat anything that comes along. This swallower, like many other deep-sea fish, has an expandable stomach that can easily stretch to hold a gigantic meal—including fish bigger than itself.

Long, trunklike snout used to search for food on the seabed

Large, well-developed eyes set high on the head

Expanded stomach can take several months to digest a particularly large meal

Small mouth filled with platelike grinding teeth

FLOATING FISH

Anglerfish larvae start life enclosed in a bubble that helps them to float close to the sea surface, where food is plentiful. When it changes into the adult form, the anglerfish migrates to the deep sea.

GHOSTLY FISH

Flabby, grayish bodies and oddly shaped heads give chimaeras such a strange appearance that they are sometimes called ghost sharks or spook fish. They are an odd group of fish, with some features of bony fish and some features of sharks. This plow-nosed chimaera is also known as the elephant fish because of its long snout. It uses the snout to plow through mud on the bottom, searching for food. In spite of its weird looks, the elephant fish is good to eat and is sought after by deep-sea trawlers.

LIVING FOSSIL

When a deep-sea trawler hauled up this stumpy, armor-plated fish in 1938, the fishermen had no idea what it was. But scientists could hardly believe their eyes—it was just as if a living dinosaur had been discovered! Many fossil coelacanths had been found in the past, but never a living specimen, so they were thought to have been extinct for millions of years.

ALL WASHED UP

This "sea serpent" was washed up on a Californian beach in 1906. It is actually a ribbonfish that probably came to the surface because it was dying. These deep-sea fish have thin, eellike bodies up to 23 ft (7 m) long. Very few have been found, so we know little about the lives of these mysterious fish.

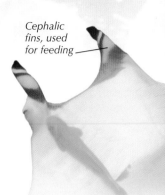

Cephalic fins, used for feeding

Large "wings" can measure 20 ft (6 m) from tip to tip

SEA MONSTERS

EARLY SEAFARERS believed that the ocean's depths were full of terrifying, dangerous monsters such as sea serpents and devilfish. Today, scientific investigation of the deep sea has given us a clearer picture of the creatures that live beneath the ocean's surface. Although many of these legendary creatures do exist, we now know that most are harmless. What all the "monsters" have in common is their sheer size. Large animals survive well in the ocean because the water supports the weight of their bodies. Some enormous sea creatures, such as the giant octopus and giant squid, do not even have a skeleton to support their huge bodies, and are soft and limp when removed from the water.

MANTA RAY

Manta rays were given the name "devilfish" because of the strange-looking horns at the front of their heads. It was thought that these were used to stun prey. In fact, the horns funnel patches of drifting plankton into the huge mouths of these gentle giants.

OCTOPUS

Some giant octopuses have been found to have an armspan of 23 ft (7 m) or more—big enough to envelop a small car. Despite their fearsome size, octopuses only prey on small fish, crabs, and other shellfish. Octopuses are intelligent, too. By teaching them to select objects by feel or sight, scientists have proved that octopuses have the ability to learn and remember.

INKY VEIL

When threatened, the giant octopus makes a backward escape using jet propulsion. It rapidly sucks water in and squirts it back out from a funnel near its mouth. Its tentacles trail out behind its body, making it streamlined so that it can swim faster. A frightened octopus may also release a smokescreen of black ink from a special sac to confuse its enemy, as shown above.

Fanciful illustration of a kraken, a creature probably based on sightings of dying giant squid at the sea's surface

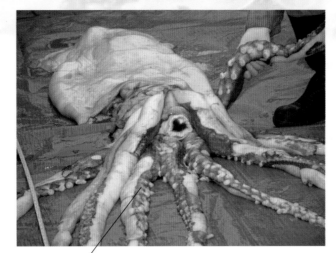

Ten tentacles, including two specialized feeding tentacles

REAL-LIFE MONSTER

The giant squid is a deep-sea monster that no one has yet seen alive. This one was caught in a fishing net off the west coast of Scotland in 2002. It measured 10 ft (3.15 m) long. The record so far is 42 ft (13 m). No wonder early sightings of this creature led to stories of the "kraken"— a many-armed monster that could sink a ship.

Actual size tooth

FEARSOME TOOTH

The great white shark's triangular, serrated teeth are designed to rip chunks out of large prey such as seals. Amazingly, sharks have several rows of teeth. When a tooth breaks, a new one quickly grows forward from the row behind.

WHITE HUNTER!

The great white shark is the largest of all predatory fish—it grows to over 20 ft (6 m) long. Special heat exchangers in the great white's blood system allow it to keep its swimming muscles warm. This means it can chase its prey at speeds of up to 25 mph (40 kmh), even in very cold water. Great whites often feed near the surface on seals and turtles, but they also hunt for fish in deep water.

LOST PALACE

A TRAVELER LONG AGO wrote of the wonders of Alexandria, the capital of ancient Egypt. Cleopatra, last of the pharaohs, had a palace on an island in the royal harbor there. But 400 years after her death, earthquakes toppled the buildings and a tidal wave swallowed up the harbor. In 1996, marine archaeologist Franck Goddio set out to search for Cleopatra's lost palace, using the latest underwater technology. In the murky waters, the divers discovered the statue of a priest and two sphinxes nearby. Experts believe that these figures stand on the site of a sacred shrine within Cleopatra's palace. Two thousand years ago, Cleopatra herself probably worshipped here.

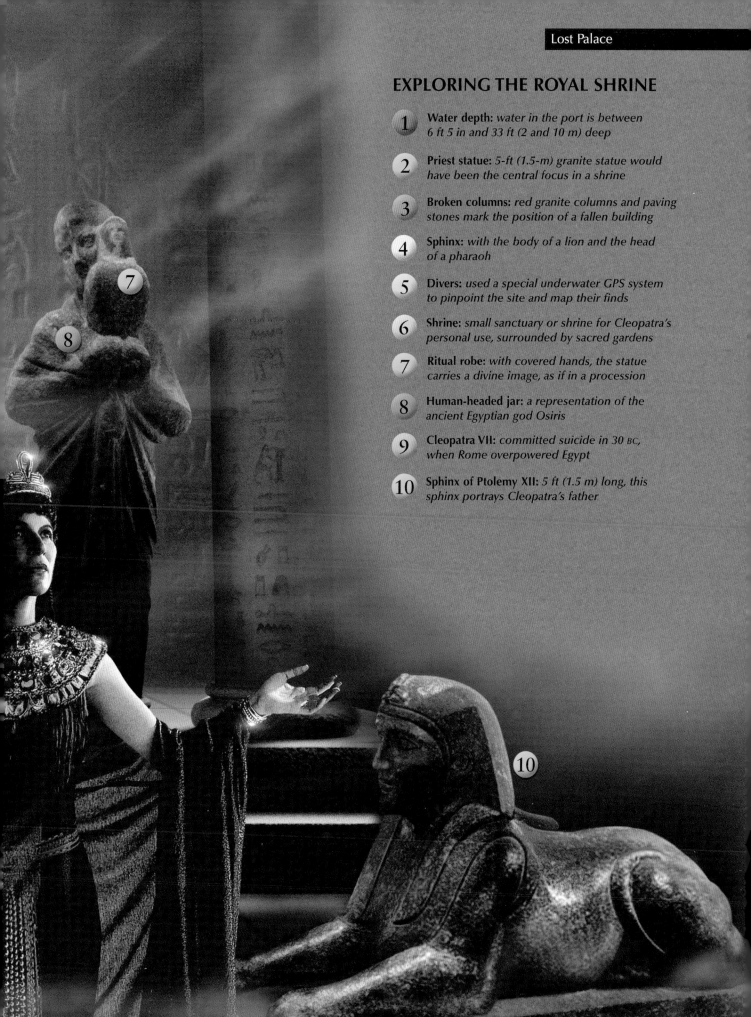

EXPLORING THE ROYAL SHRINE

1 Water depth: *water in the port is between 6 ft 5 in and 33 ft (2 and 10 m) deep*

2 Priest statue: *5-ft (1.5-m) granite statue would have been the central focus in a shrine*

3 Broken columns: *red granite columns and paving stones mark the position of a fallen building*

4 Sphinx: *with the body of a lion and the head of a pharaoh*

5 Divers: *used a special underwater GPS system to pinpoint the site and map their finds*

6 Shrine: *small sanctuary or shrine for Cleopatra's personal use, surrounded by sacred gardens*

7 Ritual robe: *with covered hands, the statue carries a divine image, as if in a procession*

8 Human-headed jar: *a representation of the ancient Egyptian god Osiris*

9 Cleopatra VII: *committed suicide in 30 BC, when Rome overpowered Egypt*

10 Sphinx of Ptolemy XII: *5 ft (1.5 m) long, this sphinx portrays Cleopatra's father*

SUBMERGED TREASURES
Before Alexandria was founded in 331 BC, Herakleion was Egypt's main port. The city is thought to have been destroyed by an earthquake, and lay buried beneath the waves for over a thousand years. It was finally discovered in June 2000 by marine archaeologist Franck Goddio.

A diver investigates a temple statue

An Egyptian stele (decorated stone slab) found in the sunken city of Herakleion

LOST AND FOUND

THE FORGOTTEN REMAINS of ancient civilizations that once flourished on coasts and islands now lie at the bottom of the sea like buried treasure, waiting to be uncovered. Some were swallowed up by volcanic eruptions, earthquakes, and tsunamis (tidal waves), and disappeared beneath the waves. Others were submerged more gradually, by rising sea levels. Today, global sea levels are rising once more and the sea may eventually engulf some low-lying areas. In the Bay of Alexandria in Egypt, it is easy to see that submerged structures are part of the ancient port. However, at other sites, such as the recently discovered Mahabalipuram in India, it is unclear whether the structures are artificial or natural.

A bronze statue of Poseidon, the Greek god of the sea

In some accounts, Atlantis was built on a series of ringlike islands

POSEIDON
Legend has it that the Greek god of the sea, Poseidon, founded the city of Atlantis. The city was said to be one of the most peaceful, beautiful, and prosperous places in the world, until it sank beneath the waves during a catastrophic earthquake.

ATLANTIS
No one knows whether Atlantis ever existed. One theory is that Atlantis was an island called Thera, near Crete, that was devastated by a volcano. In 1883, the Indonesian island of Krakatoa disappeared beneath the waves when the volcano it was sitting on erupted.

WARMING UP

Most scientists now agree that the Earth's climate is getting warmer, leading to warmer oceans and rising sea levels. Most of the sea-level rise is because warmer water takes up more space than cold water.

Melting glaciers have so far contributed only a little extra water

This flat island in the Maldives rises very little above the surrounding sea level

FLOOD WARNING

Low-lying islands perched on top of coral reefs, such as the Maldives in the Indian Ocean, could eventually be submerged if sea levels continue to rise. Global warming also means that storms are getting worse in some areas. Bangladesh has been built on a huge river delta, and stormy seas are causing increased flooding.

SHORE TEMPLE AT MAHABALIPURAM

Old stories are often the starting point for explorers trying to find a lost city. According to legend, there were once seven temples on the shore near Mahabalipuram on India's east coast. All but one were submerged by waves thrown up by angry gods. This temple standing alone on the shore may be a surviving part of the ancient city.

Foundation stones of ancient temples, or natural rock formations?

EXPEDITION MAHABALIPURAM

On April 1, 2002, a team of divers from India and England made their first dive to find the ruins of this lost city. What they found were huge stone blocks, covered in seaweed and silt and scattered over several square miles.

MARINE TOURISM

In the Caribbean, tourists can now observe shallow ocean habitats without getting wet. Submersibles such as *Atlantis Deep Explorer* carry passengers to depths of around 100 ft (30 m) to view colorful soft corals and other ocean creatures. Soon tourists may be able to visit the deep ocean—for a price—just as the first tourists have visited space.

Barnacles
attached to the outside of the can

NEW HABITATS

WHEN A HARD OBJECT is left in the sea for any length of time, living marine growths gradually cover it until it is indistinguishable from the natural underwater environment. Creatures such as anemones, corals, and sponges spend most of their lives firmly attached to the seabed, but these plantlike animals start life as tiny larvae that drift with the ocean currents. For these larvae looking for new living space, a shipwreck or the legs of an oil rig are just as good as a rock. Holes and crevices on wrecks are soon home to crabs, lobsters, octopuses, and small fish. Even a whale carcass can become an animal habitat.

HOME FOR GOBIES

Huge amounts of trash find their way into the ocean—plastic, bottles, fishing nets, and oil drums. Although garbage is often dangerous to marine wildlife, it can sometimes be useful, too. To these yellow gobies, an old tin can makes as good a home as a hole in the rocks.

Strong, sensitive suckers cover the octopus' eight tentacles

Octopus tentacles emerging from a jar

OCTOPUS IN A JAR

This diver, examining a shipwreck in the Mediterranean known as the *Glass Wreck*, must have been surprised when a large octopus wriggled out of a jar. Octopuses can squeeze their boneless bodies into very small holes. They often lay their eggs in artificial objects like this, then stay to protect the eggs until they hatch. The *Glass Wreck* octopus became the expedition's mascot and was nicknamed "Fred."

The *Mare* one month after sinking

The same ship 15 months after sinking

GOING, GOING, GONE

These two photographs, taken about a year apart, show how quickly marine life can colonize a shipwreck. In the second picture, the name of the wreck has completely disappeared—plankton containing the larvae of sponges, sea squirts, barnacles, and oysters has drifted over the wreck, and all those creatures have settled and grown there. This wreck sank in the shallow Arabian Gulf, but wrecks in the deep sea become overgrown much more slowly.

Steps
to top of mast

A BONY HOME

Most dead sea creatures are eaten long before they reach the deep-sea floor. However, dead whales sometimes sink into the depths, and very soon become a temporary home for scavenging fish. This carcass, 5,500 ft (1,670 m) down off the coast near Los Angeles, California, has been stripped to the bone. Even after the flesh is gone, many animals stay and live on among the bones, until they, too, finally disappear.

Whale vertebra

Eellike hagfish

ARTIFICIAL REEF

Encrusting animals such as corals usually grow better on the upper parts of shipwrecks than on the hull. This is because the sides and bottom of a ship are covered with "anti-fouling" paint to stop animals from settling on it. The mast of this Japanese wreck from World War II has developed into an artificial reef that now attracts many small fish.

NEW LIFE FORMS

IN 1977, SCIENTISTS exploring the seabed in
the very deepest part of the oceans made an
incredible discovery—groups of huge chimney-
like structures, dotted along a mid-ocean ridge.
These "black smokers," or hydrothermal vents,
spew out hot water thick with minerals from
beneath the ocean floor. As the vents develop, they
come to support an astonishing variety of life—but
not life as we know it. Other animals get their energy
from sunlight, through a food chain that starts with
plants converting sunlight into energy. Down here,
though, far from any sunlight or plants, the food
chain starts with bacteria that convert chemicals in
the vent water into energy. Scientists wonder if this
deep-sea soup is where life first began.

HYDROTHERMAL HOTSPOTS
Black smokers were first found in the eastern Pacific, along
the Galápagos Rift. Many more exist, mostly on rifts and
ridges where the ocean floor is spreading. The largest group,
as big as a football field, is TAG (Trans-Atlantic
Geotraverse), on the Mid-Atlantic Ridge.

EXPLORING DEEP-SEA VENTS

1 **Submersible:** *the only way to visit vents at depths of 6,500–10,000 ft (2,000– 3,000 m)*

2 **Smoke:** *the plume of minerals released by vent water at up to 650°F (350°C) when it hits seawater at around 35°F (2°C)*

3 **Chimney:** *built up gradually from minerals deposited by the vent water—the tallest so far is "Godzilla," at 160 ft (48 m)*

4 **Hot water:** *seawater seeps through Earth's crust, is heated by hot volcanic rock half a mile (1 km) below, and gushes back up*

5 **Pompeii worms:** *live in small tubes around the top of the chimney, just a few inches from the super-hot vent water*

6 **Grenadier or rattail:** *a fish that feeds on anything it can find*

7 **Giant tubeworms:** *collect chemicals from the water with their red gills—to be turned into food by bacteria inside them— and grow to 6 ft 6 in (2 m) long*

8 **Eel pout:** *some species of this eellike fish are only found at vent sites*

9 **Vent crab:** *feeds by scavenging on broken tubeworms*

10 **Giant clams:** *grow to around 10 in (25 cm) long, using food produced by bacteria in their gills*

PILLOW LAVA

Lava welling up from cracks in the ocean floor cannot flow away as it would on land. When hot lava meets cold seawater deep in the ocean, it solidifies into wrinkled mounds that look like squeezed-out toothpaste or rounded pillows. This photograph shows lava that has oozed into the sea from a volcanic island.

A fountain of lava explodes from a fissure eruption in Krafla, Iceland, which lasted from 1975 to 1984

RESTLESS OCEANS

D OWN ON THE OCEAN FLOOR, the plates that make up the Earth's crust are on the move. As the ocean plates move apart, molten lava flows up to fill the cracks, creating an underwater mountain range or "mid-ocean ridge." Where the expanding ocean plates meet a continental plate, the ocean plate is forced down into the Earth's mantle. This creates a deep trench, such as the 36,197-ft (11,033-m) Mariana Trench in the western Pacific, and a line of volcanic activity such as the "Ring of Fire" around the Pacific Ocean. We only become aware of these restless movements beneath the oceans when an underwater volcano breaks the surface or a destructive tsunami sweeps across the coast.

FISSURE ERUPTIONS

An underwater mountain range called the Mid-Atlantic Ridge runs along the deepest part of the Atlantic Ocean, marking one of the fault lines where Earth's ocean plates are pulling apart. In Iceland, the Mid-Atlantic Ridge rises just above sea level. This gives some insight into how new ocean floor is created as Earth's plates part, form long cracks called fissures, and fill with lava.

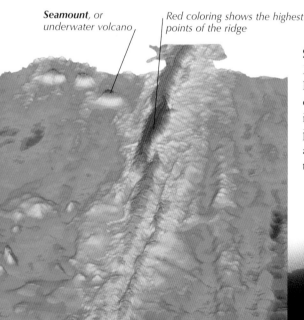

Seamount, or underwater volcano

Red coloring shows the highest points of the ridge

SONAR IMAGING

Mid-ocean ridges, such as the Pacific Rise seen here snaking along the floor of the Pacific Ocean, show up clearly in sonar maps. The ridges mark the junctions between sea floor plates, and are volcanically active along their length.

GALÁPAGOS VOLCANO

There may be as many as 10,000 submarine
volcanoes or seamounts throughout the
world, although most of them are
extinct. When seamounts break
the surface, they form volcanic
islands. These may
eventually disappear
below the surface as
waves wear them
down or as the sea
level rises.

Chinese Hats, a group
of volcanoes in the
Galápagos Islands,
eastern Pacific

Crater of extinct volcano

Cone built up from
solidified lava

TSUNAMI

Earthquakes or eruptions on the ocean floor can send a shockwave
through the water. In the open ocean, the wave, called a tsunami, is
less than 3 ft (1 m) high, but as it nears the coast, it grows up to 33 ft
(10 m) high. This wall of water crashes onto the shore, leaving terror
and devastation in its wake, as in Hawaii after this tsunami in 1960.

MANGANESE NODULES
Scattered over the ocean floor lie rocky lumps called manganese nodules that contain valuable metals such as manganese, copper, and nickel. They take millions of years to grow from deposits of chemicals dissolved in the seawater. Scientists are looking at ways to harvest the metals without damaging the deep-sea environment.

DEEP FLIGHT
Although modern submersibles can safely carry scientists down to at least 4 miles (6.5 km), they are difficult to maneuver underwater. *Deep Flight* is a new type of submersible, designed to "fly" through the water by using movable wings and battery-powered thrusters. Future versions may one day be capable of full ocean depth.

DRILLING BIT
To extract samples of rock and sediment from the seabed, geologists use different types of drilling heads, or bits, depending on the structure of the rock, how deep they want to drill, and whether they want fragments of rock or a long core.

SEA RESEARCH

FROM THE SHALLOW margins of the sea, known as the continental shelf, people harvest a huge variety of resources—food, medicines, minerals, and even energy. However, as some of these resources begin to grow scarce, attention is turning more and more to the deep. Geologists are drilling into the deep-sea bed to search for oil, gas, and minerals, and to find out more about how the oceans work. New types of submersibles may eventually carry marine biologists to the deepest depths to study the life forms there. Much of the specialized equipment that scientists need to investigate this environment was first developed by the oil and communications industries to lay and maintain their deep-sea pipelines and cables.

Water may be over 26,000 ft (8,000 m) deep

Pods provide panoramic visibility and have underwater telephones for communication

DRILLING SHIP
Geological ships are held in position by computer-controlled thrusters, while their drilling equipment bites into the seabed. The ocean floor is covered with layers of sediment, made up of mud, sand, and silt washed off the land, and layers of ooze formed by the remains of dead marine plants and animals. Scientists can calculate the age of the ocean floor by studying the depth and structure of these layers.

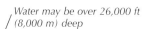

Reentry cone marks position of drill hole for later missions

Layers of sediment and rock

UNDERWATER MAINTENANCE

Pipelines like this carry oil and gas ashore from drilling rigs. While most pipelines are now checked remotely by computers, specialized diving suits and tools such as this rotary cleaning brush have been developed to help divers maintain the pipelines.

CABLES

Welding is just one of the repair and maintenance tasks that can be carried out on deep-sea cables and pipelines by submersibles such as *Deep Rover*. The first transatlantic telephone cable was laid in 1866, and soon the oceans were crisscrossed by a vast network of cables. Today, satellites have largely taken over the job, making many of these cables obsolete.

Lightweight frame *makes* Deep Flight *easy to maneuver*

Aerodynamic shape *helps* Deep Flight *travel quickly through the water*

Manipulators *are used to weld cables underwater*

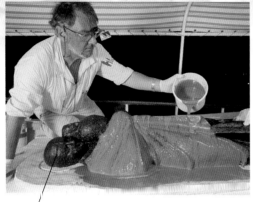

MAKING MOLDS

Artists made exact copies of artifacts from the sunken remains at Alexandria, so that experts around the world could study them. First, liquid silicon was poured over the object. When this had set, a thick resin was added, to keep the mold rigid. Molds were made in two halves, then filled to create a "cast" or replica.

A layer of petroleum jelly protects the statue from the red silicon

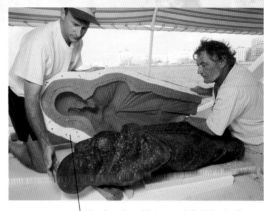

The hard mold is carefully lifted off

DEEP-SEA ALERT

THE ONCE-MYSTERIOUS deep-sea world is more accessible today, thanks to modern technology. But technology has also led to damage and exploitation. Pipelines and cables crisscross the ocean floor, pollution seeps out from tanker wrecks, and the fishing industry is threatening the delicate deep-sea ecosystem. The oceans' resources are essential to us, but not inexhaustible, and steps must be taken to protect and manage them. Creating marine reserves and even underwater museums is one way forward—the submerged port of Alexandria may in time become a museum, which visitors could reach with diving gear or in submersibles.

RETURN TO THE SEA

Artifacts from Alexandria, such as this statue of a priest, were removed for casting and then returned to the seabed. Accurate GPS records enabled Franck Goddio and his team of divers to replace each object in its exact original position.

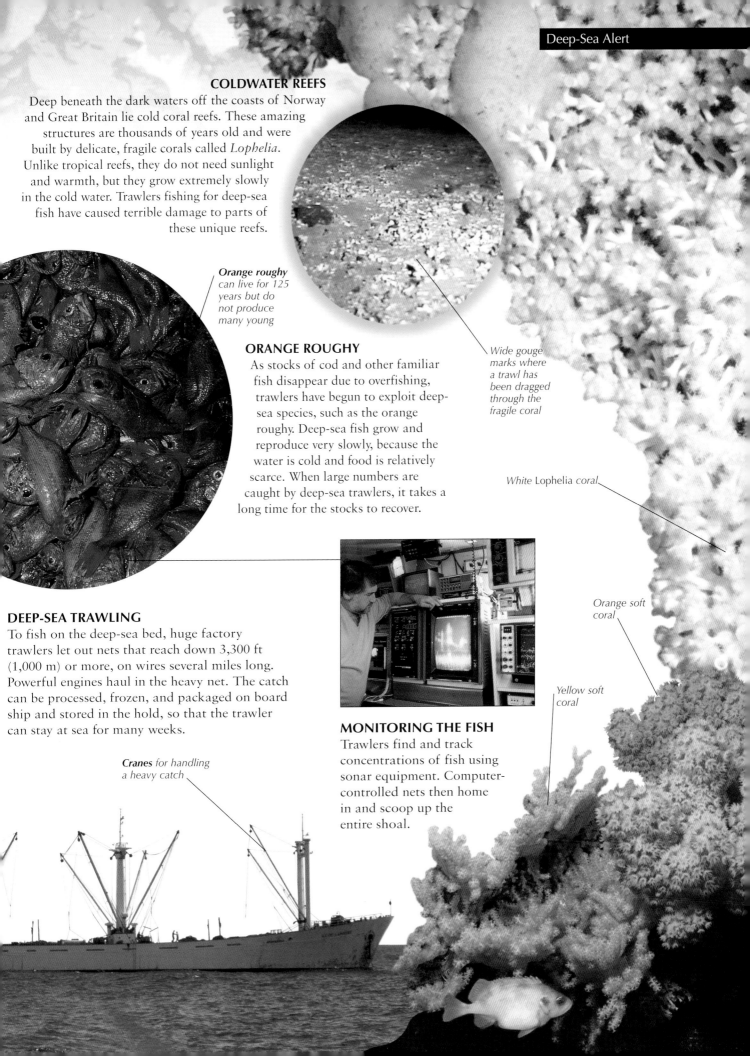

COLDWATER REEFS

Deep beneath the dark waters off the coasts of Norway and Great Britain lie cold coral reefs. These amazing structures are thousands of years old and were built by delicate, fragile corals called *Lophelia*. Unlike tropical reefs, they do not need sunlight and warmth, but they grow extremely slowly in the cold water. Trawlers fishing for deep-sea fish have caused terrible damage to parts of these unique reefs.

Orange roughy can live for 125 years but do not produce many young

Wide gouge marks where a trawl has been dragged through the fragile coral

ORANGE ROUGHY

As stocks of cod and other familiar fish disappear due to overfishing, trawlers have begun to exploit deep-sea species, such as the orange roughy. Deep-sea fish grow and reproduce very slowly, because the water is cold and food is relatively scarce. When large numbers are caught by deep-sea trawlers, it takes a long time for the stocks to recover.

White Lophelia *coral*

Orange soft coral

DEEP-SEA TRAWLING

To fish on the deep-sea bed, huge factory trawlers let out nets that reach down 3,300 ft (1,000 m) or more, on wires several miles long. Powerful engines haul in the heavy net. The catch can be processed, frozen, and packaged on board ship and stored in the hold, so that the trawler can stay at sea for many weeks.

Yellow soft coral

MONITORING THE FISH

Trawlers find and track concentrations of fish using sonar equipment. Computer-controlled nets then home in and scoop up the entire shoal.

Cranes for handling a heavy catch

INDEX

ACKNOWLEDGEMENTS

Dorling Kindersley would like to thank:
Franck Goddio, Harbor Branch Oceanographic Institution, Inc. and Woods Hole Oceanographic Institution for technical details, Andy Crawford for photography, Stefan Podhorodecki and Marie Spiers for modelling, Hilary Bird for the index

The publisher would like to thank the following for their kind permission to reproduce their photographs.
Key: a-above; b-below; c-centre; l-left; r-right; t-top; Ace-Acetate

AKG London: Erich Lessing 26bc; Peter Connolly 26crb. **AMNH:** 7cra; Charlestown Shipwreck Heritage Centre 12cla. © Christie's Images Ltd: 12cb. **Corbis:** Amos Nachoum 5cla, 13ca, 19br; Brandon D Cole 3t, 4t-5t, 38; Charles and Josette Lenars 27cl; Jeffrey L Rotman 31 Ace bl; Jonathan Blair endpapers, 5tr,

6-7, 10-11, 12-13, 13tr, 13cl, 13bc, 14tl, 14-15, 26cl; Michael S Yamashita 36-37; NASA 33tr; Ralph White 8ca, 10tl, 10tr, 10cb, 10bl, 15cra, 17bc, 30ca; Ralph White/NOAA 31ca, 30 Ace, 31 Ace cra; Rick Price 20cl; Roger Ressmeyer 5bl, 35bc; Stuart Westmorland 23br; W M Horton 22tl. **Cyberflix:** 9cr, 9 Ace cl. **University of Delaware College of Marine Studies:** 31 Ace cr. **Dr Frances Dipper:** 29cla, 29cl. **Fortean Picture Library:** 23cla. **Franck Goddio\Hilti Foundation:** 5cr, 24bl, 24br, 24 Ace bl, 24 Ace br, 24 Ace c, 24 Ace cl, 25cla, 25br, 25 Ace bl, 36cla, 36bl; 26tl, 26tr. **Jason Hall Spencer:** 37br. **HBOI:** 7cla. **Institute of Marine Research:** 37tcr. **Jamstec:** 19tc. **Katz/FSP:** 12crb; Gamma 11bc; Wilson/Liaison/ Gamma 34-35. **Liverpool Maritime Museum:** 4-5. **Richard A Lutz:** 31bc, 31 (eel pout). **The Mary Rose Trust:** 14bl, 14tra. **Masterfile UK:** Bill Brooks

27cra; Ron Stroud 27ca. **National Marine Aquarium:** Carol Hicks 23ca. N.H.P.A.: ANT 20-21; Henry Ausloos 3cb; Norbert Wu 16-17, 16 Ace cr, 16 Ace cra, 17 Ace, 18tl, 21tr. **Nature Picture Library Ltd:** Constantinos Petrinos 26-27, 28-29; David Shale 7tc; Florian Graner 37tl; Jeff Rotman 22cr, 22bl; Jeff Rotman 22-23. **NOAA:** 16 Ace bl, 16 Ace clb. **Ocean Drilling Programme:** John Tenison 34cla. **Oceanworks International Corporation:** 18-19. **Onslows Titanic Picture Library:** 11c. **OSF:** Hjalmar Bardarson 32cra; Kim Westerskov 37cl, 37cr; Norbert Wu 20cb, 21cr; Rudie Kuiter 20clb. **Pacific Tsunami Museum:** 33cr. **Popperfoto:** 11cb. **Rex Features:** 11cr; Zena Holloway 18clb. **RMS Titanic Inc.:** 8 Ace. **RNLI:** 6tr. **Santha Hancock:** Seapics.com: David Wrobel 20tl; Doug Perrine 28tl; Gregory Ochocki 17cla, 17 Ace17; James D Watt 32tl; Mako Hirose 28cra; Mako Hirose 29tr. **SPL:** 15cla, 34bl; B Murton/Southampton Oceanography Centre 32-33; David Parker 15tl; Dr Ken Macdonal 32bl;

Dynamic Earth Imaging 6cb; Institute of Oceanographic Sciences/NERC 34tl; Institute of Oceanographic Sciences/NERC/USGS 7cb; Matthew Shipp 32-33; MURA/Jerrican 35tr; Peter Scoones 6tl, 18-19, 20-21, 21cr, 22-23; Southampton Oceanography Centre 34-35; W Haxby Lamont-Doherty Earth Observatory 15bc. **Prof Craig R Smith:** C Smith & M. DeGruy 29bc. **Woods Hole Oceanographic Instititution:** 8cra, 8cl, 16 Ace main image, 16 Ace clb; Holger Jannasch 31 Ace cbl.

Jacket credits: Front: Seapics.com: Gregory Ochocki. **Back:** Corbis: Alese & Mort Pechter t. Jonathan Blair tl. **Seapics.com:** Doug Perrine tc. **Spine:** The Miami Herald/Chuck Sadely.

All other images © Dorling Kindersley. For further information see: www.dkimages.com

Every effort has been made to trace copyright holders of photographs. The publishers apologise for any omissions.